ALFRED's
SACRED PERFORMER
COLLECTIONS

LATE INTERMEDIATE TO EARLY ADVANCED PIANO

What *Praise* Can I Play on Sunday?

Book 1: January and February Services

10 Easily Prepared Arrangements

Arranged by Carol Tornquist

I have been a church pianist from a very young age, playing various styles of music from classical pieces, to hymns, to gospel songs. By the time I became involved in Christian music publishing as an arranger, praise music was emerging as the most popular musical expression of worship. Its singable melodies and catchy rhythms produced a musical style accessible to musicians and congregations alike. Today, praise songs are being sung and listened to not only on Sunday mornings but practically anytime and anywhere.

In creating this series, I have chosen the best praise songs, and they are recognizable to most congregations. Each arrangement is easy to prepare and tastefully arranged in a contemporary style appropriate for Sunday morning worship services. Book 1, for January and February, features solos for Epiphany, Creation, Transfiguration, Ash Wednesday, and Lent as well as general (non-seasonal) selections. Other books in this series are as follows:

Book 2: March and April
Book 3: May and June
Book 4: July and August

Book 5: September and October
Book 6: November and December

I hope pianists will find this series to be a perfect all-in-one resource for the entire church year.

Carol Tornquist

Produced by
Alfred Music Publishing Co., Inc.
P.O. Box 10003
Van Nuys, CA 91410-0003
alfred.com

Printed in USA.

ISBN-10: 0-7390-8405-4
ISBN-13: 978-0-7390-8405-2
Cover Photo: © iStockphoto.com/mycola

(Approx. Performance Time – 2:15)
General

Come, Now Is the Time to Worship

Words and Music by Brian Doerksen
Arranged by Carol Tornquist

Reflectively (♩ = 52)

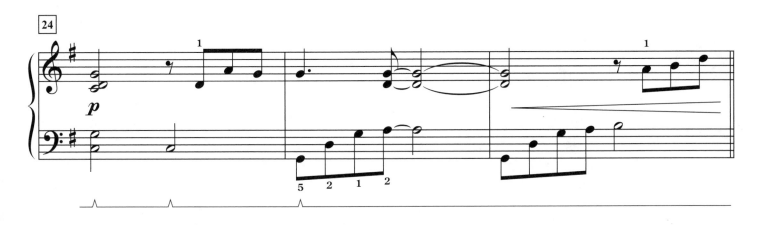

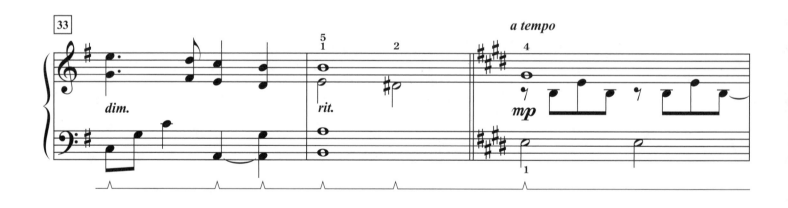

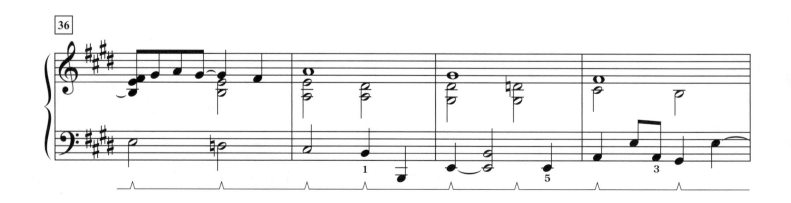

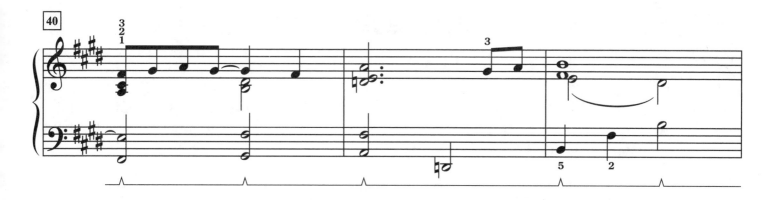

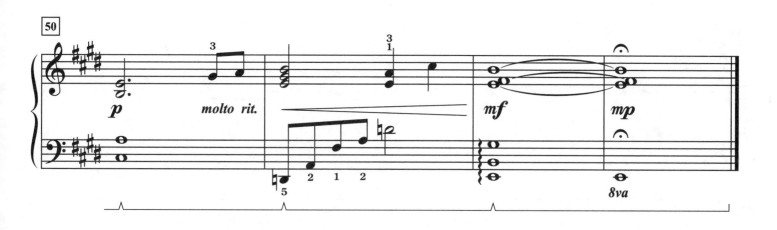

(Approx. Performance Time – 2:00)
General

Off 3/31/14

Forever

Words and Music by Chris Tomlin
Arranged by Carol Tornquist

Moderately, in two ($\frac{}{}$ = 58)

Start affeculous 3/31/14

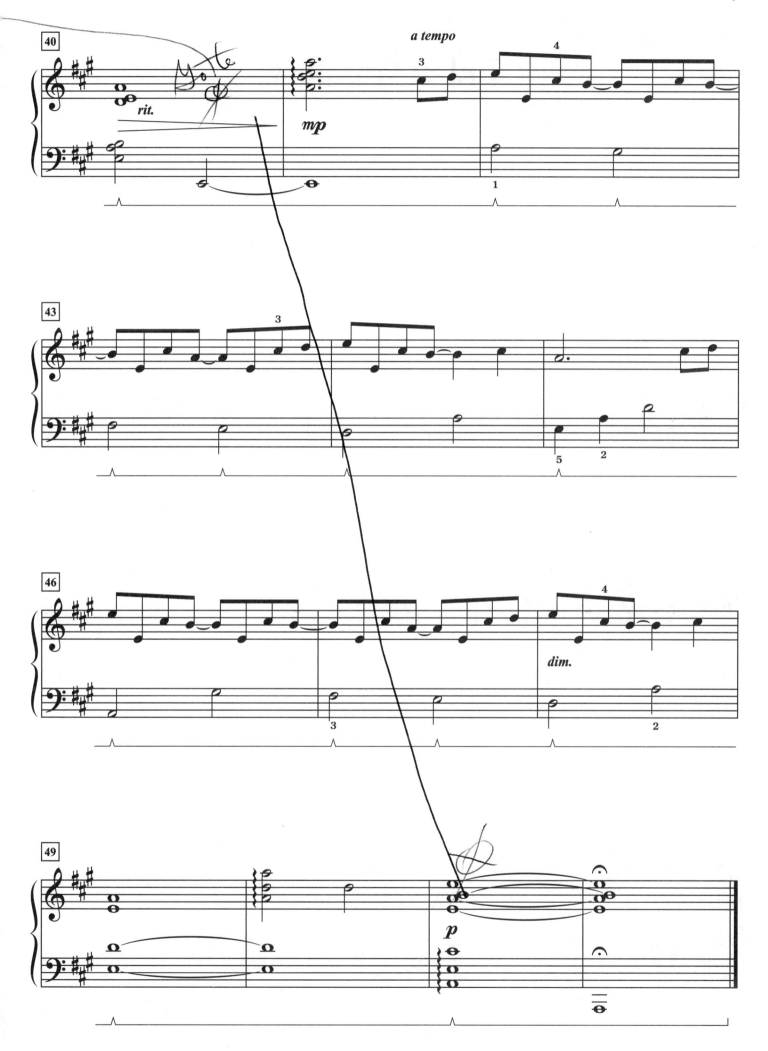

3/16/14
7/20/14

(Approx. Performance Time – 2:45)
Creation / General

God of Wonders

Words and Music by
Marc Byrd and Steve Hindalong
Arranged by Carol Tornquist

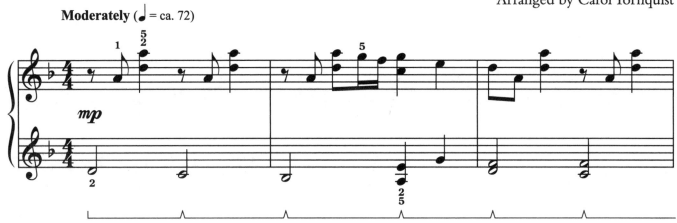

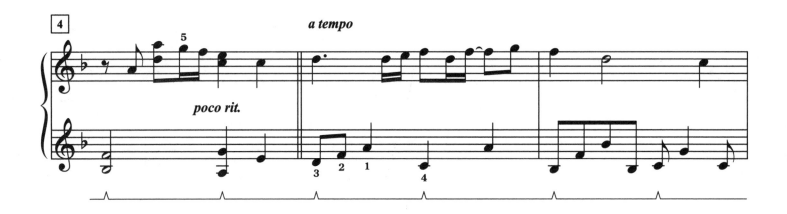

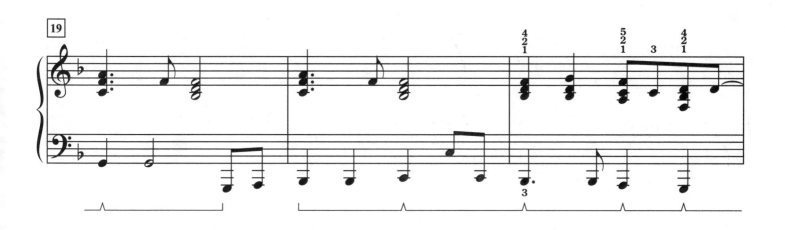

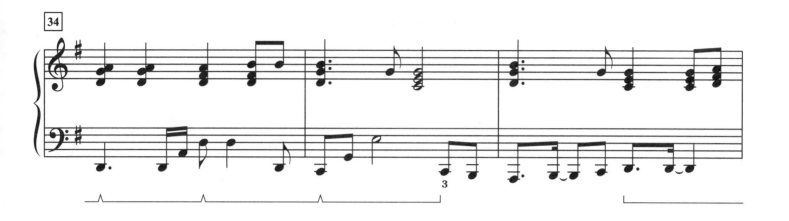

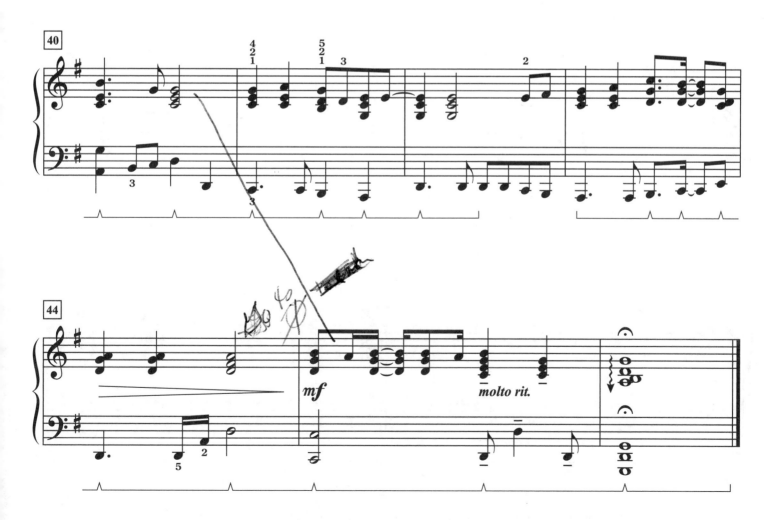

(Approx. Performance Time – 2:15)

Transfiguration/General

Hosanna

(Praise Is Rising)

Words and Music by
Brenton Brown and Paul Baloche
Arranged by Carol Tornquist

(Approx. Performance Time – 3:30)
Lent

How Deep the Father's Love for Us

Words and Music by Stuart Townend
Arranged by Carol Tornquist

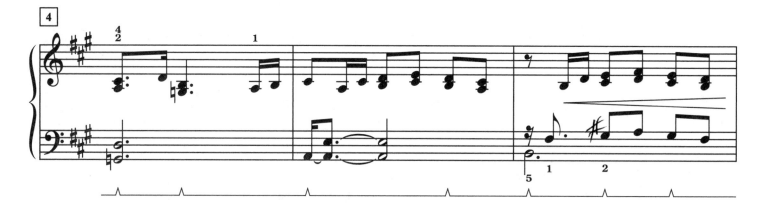

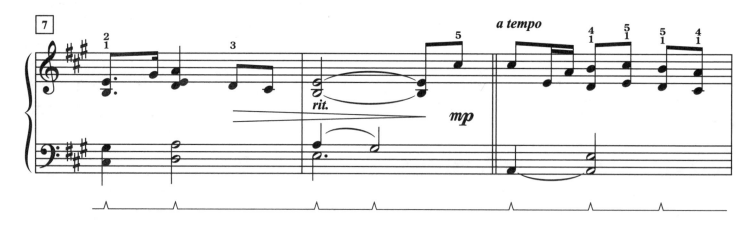

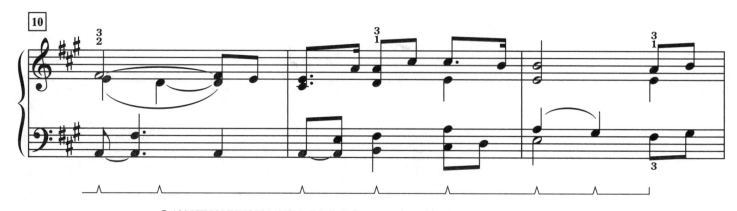

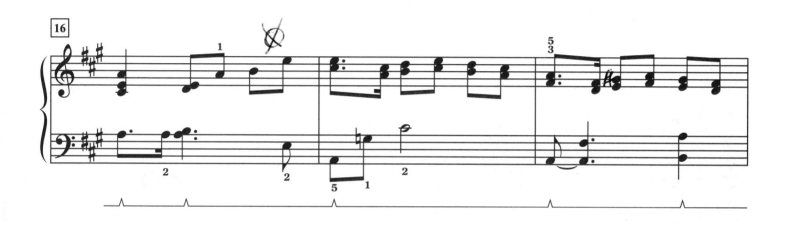

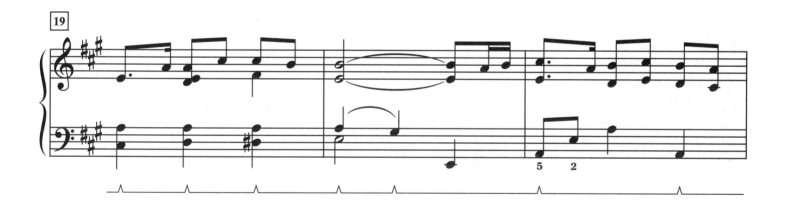

(Approx. Performance Time – 2:30)
Creation/General

How Great Is Our God

Words and Music by
Jesse Reeves, Chris Tomlin and Ed Cash
Arranged by Carol Tornquist

With confidence (♩ = ca. 92)

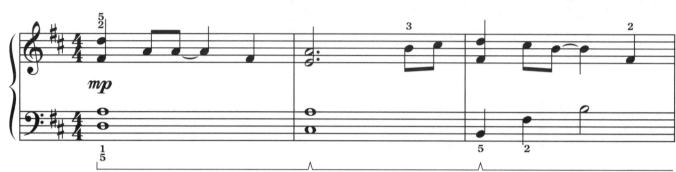

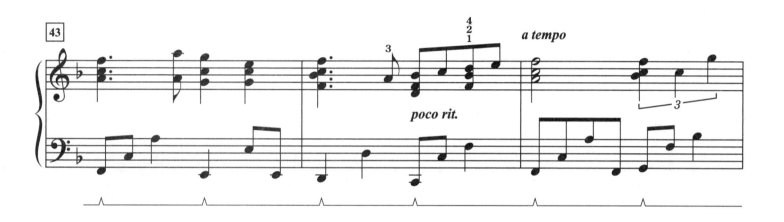

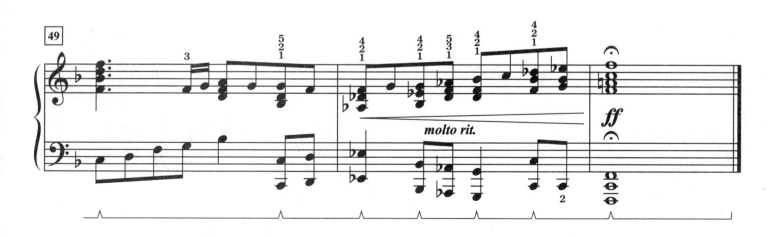

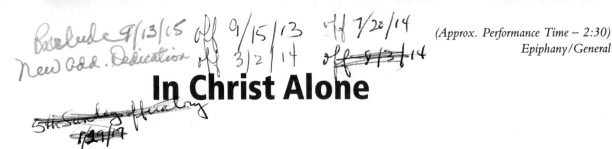

(Approx. Performance Time – 2:30)
Epiphany/General

In Christ Alone

Words and Music by
Stuart Townend and Keith Getty
Arranged by Carol Tornquist

Not hurried, with rubato (♩ = ca. 72)

25 **Freely and expressively**

16th notes

28

31

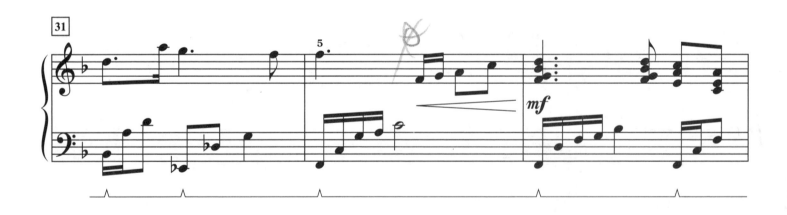

34

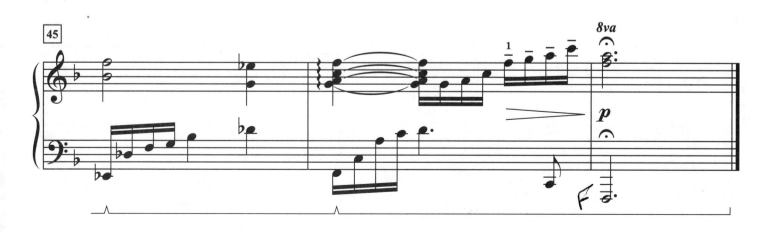

(Approx. Performance Time – 2:15)
General

Majesty

(Here I Am)

Words and Music by
Martin Smith and Stuart Garrard
Arranged by Carol Tornquist

You Are My All in All

Words and Music by Dennis L. Jernigan
Arranged by Carol Tornquist

Flowing (♩. = ca. 60)

(Approx. Performance Time – 2:45)
Lent/Ash Wednesday

The Wonderful Cross

Words and Music by
Chris Tomlin, J.D. Walt and Jesse Reeves
Arranged by Carol Tornquist

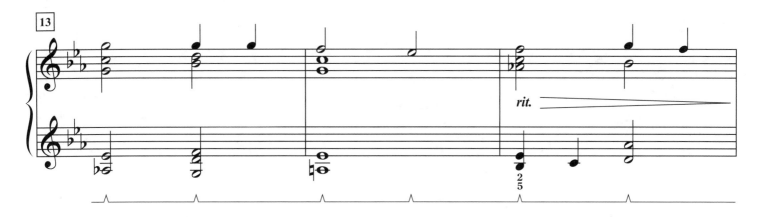

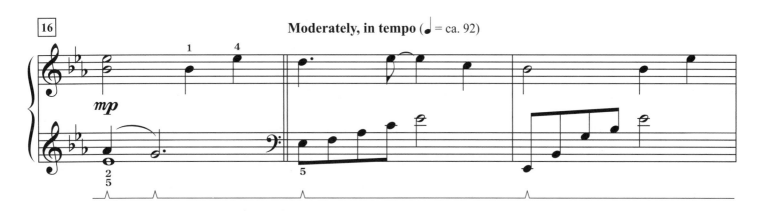

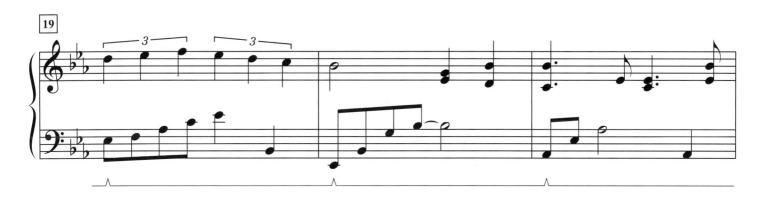